Original title:
Tales of the Timberland

Copyright © 2025 Creative Arts Management OÜ
All rights reserved.

Author: Gabriel Kingsley
ISBN HARDBACK: 978-1-80567-169-5
ISBN PAPERBACK: 978-1-80567-468-9

Voices Carried by the Winds

In the woods where whispers play,
Squirrels chatter all the day.
They bicker over nuts and seeds,
While raccoons plot their midnight deeds.

A wise old owl hoots with flair,
"Who stole my snack? That's just not fair!"
The breeze joins in, a playful sound,
Carrying laughter, all around.

The Spirit of the Timber Trails

Mice in boots, all marching right,
Leading a parade, oh what a sight!
Hats on hedgehogs, straws in paws,
They dance beneath the bear's applause.

A porcupine plays the sax so well,
His tunes echo, a forest spell.
While fireflies light the nightly show,
They twirl and twist, put on a glow.

Mysteries of the Maple Grove

In the grove where the syrup flows,
Ants hold meetings, sharing woes.
"Why is the maple syrup sticky?"
A wise old tree replies, "How tricky!"

Bears take bets on the best gold leaf,
While chipmunks scheme in disbelief.
They giggle as the squirrels engage,
In a nutty plotting rampage.

Tales from the Underbrush

Down below where the shadows peek,
Bunnies gossip, sharing the cheek.
"Did you see that fox in the hat?"
"Oh please, he looked just like a brat!"

A hedgehog rolls by, takes a dash,
His bowtie flies as he makes a splash.
The ferns all sway to the rhythm they make,
In this wild party, no one's awake!

Voices of the Seasons' Change

The trees all gossip as winds go by,
One claims it's winter, the next says, 'Nigh!'
Squirrels are chattering, plotting their play,
'Is it summer yet? We wish it would stay!'

The flowers giggle with colors so bright,
'Is that a snowflake? Oh no, what a fright!'
Leaves dance like dancers, twirling in cheer,
Each season's a show, with laughter we hear.

Reflections in the Crystal Pond

The pond tells secrets, as frogs like to croak,
'I'll give you a riddle,' a wise old toad spoke.
'Why did the lily never learn how to swim?'
'Because it was too lily, and not very slim!'

Fish flip and flop, making splashes of fun,
'Watch me do backflips, I'm the number one!'
The dragonflies giggle as they dart and dive,
'Life's just a game, we all feel alive.'

Nature's Palette in Autumn Hues

The leaves are laughing, in colors they boast,
Yellows and reds, they dance like a host.
'Catch me if you can!' a maple leaf shouts,
While acorns roll by with snickers and grouts.

A pumpkin grins wide, with a silly big face,
'I'm here for the party, let's pick up the pace!'
They all join together, in a wild, wacky spree,
Autumn's a painter, and everyone's free.

The Burden of Ancient Oaks

Old oaks are wise, but they tend to complain,
'Back in my day, it never did rain!'
Their branches are heavy with stories untold,
Yet under their shade, lies laughter, so bold.

'Why do you stand there, you big, grumpy tree?'
The saplings all giggle, 'You're our family!'
With roots intertwined, they share tons of glee,
Even the owls know, they're all family.

Beneath the Twilight Treetops

Squirrels in capes, they plan their heist,
Gathering acorns, oh so precise.
Under the glow of the setting sun,
Laughter erupts as their antics run.

A raccoon in glasses reads a map,
Searching for snacks in an old trash gap.
Owls chuckle softly in feathered coats,
As mischief unfolds on woodland notes.

The Voice of the Wildflowers

Daisies gossip, with petals so bright,
Sharing secrets of the moonlight.
Sunflowers dance in a whimsical spree,
Waving to bees, 'Come buzz with me!'

Buttercups giggle, their blooms all aglow,
Marigolds wink, putting on a show.
In this floral forum, with colors so bold,
Every bloom tales of fun to be told.

Whims of the Wandering Wind

The wind plays tricks, with a cheeky grin,
Tugging at hats, oh where to begin?
It swirls up high and tickles down low,
Chasing loose leaves in a lively flow.

It steals a kite, gives it a spin,
Twirling and swirling, let the fun begin!
In a wild race 'round the towering trees,
The wind whispers secrets, a playful tease.

Rooted in Reverie

Old trees sit tall, with wisdom to share,
Chortling softly, they don't have a care.
With roots deep down, they chuckle with glee,
At the antics of critters who dance 'round the tree.

They've seen it all, the joy and the strife,
Squirrels who slip in their delightful life.
In the shade of their branches, mischief abounds,
As laughter and friendship echo the grounds.

Dreaming Among the Pines

In the forest, squirrels tease,
From lofty branches, they do sneeze.
Bouncing acorns, laughter loud,
The clever fox pranks every crowd.

Beneath the boughs, birds take wing,
Chasing shadows, they chirp and sing.
Dancing leaves in playful swirl,
Nature's antics make hearts twirl.

A bear in shades, quite the sight,
Sips from a stream, feeling light.
Pinecone hats on rabbits' heads,
Comic scenes in peaceful beds.

Dreams collide with sunlight's gleam,
In this woods, all faces beam.
Wacky critters, every kind,
Joyful mishaps, oh, how they bind!

Legends Etched in Bark

On tree trunks, stories flow,
Carved by squirrels, don't you know?
A turtle once raced a fleet hare,
Claimed victory with casual flair.

Owls gossip around the glade,
"Did you see the parade made?"
Woodpeckers tap a rhythm so fine,
Beats that could make a rock star shine.

Raccoons hosting their starry night,
Dancing wildly, what a sight!
The moon winks, joining the show,
A legend begins with a quirky glow.

Graffiti art in nature's hall,
Every creature's a part of the call.
Whimsical tales, wild and free,
Etched in bark, the forest's glee.

The Nomads of the Wilderness

A deer with shades on strolled by,
Sipping nectar, oh so spry.
Frogs on lily pads all croaked,
Tales of travelers, all happily joked.

Forests echo with hoots and wails,
While raccoons plan their funny trails.
With backpacks made from leaves and vines,
Adventure awaits on playful lines.

Wanderers in the cool night air,
Finding snacks without a care.
The ants tell stories, oh what fun!
A picnic feast that's never done.

Sunrise brings a giggling crowd,
Creatures mingle, feeling proud.
Nomads rove, 'neath skies so blue,
In this wild realm, laughter renews.

Beneath the Boughs of Time

Whispers tickle the leaves so green,
Nuts and berries share the scene.
Squirrels plot their next big heist,
Peanut butter toast, oh, how nice!

The owl, wise, wears glasses round,
Correcting tales that twirl around.
A hedgehog offers sage advice,
"Life's too short, just roll the dice!"

Under boughs, where life erupts,
Nature's fabric, laughter disrupts.
Every creature, a storyteller bold,
In this wood, memories unfold.

Through seasons, the humor's spun,
As animals bask in the sun.
Rich with smiles, old friends align,
Beneath the boughs, the world's divine.

Whispers of the Woodland

In the forest, squirrels plot,
Gathering nuts, tying a knot.
With acorns dropped, a loud sound,
Befuddled, the owl spins round.

Rabbits dance with shoes too tight,
Hopping left, then taking flight.
They giggle in their furry coats,
As owls burst into silly notes.

Badgers grumble, gruff and loud,
While waving to a passing cloud.
"Hey there, friend! Mind your speed!"
Then trip on roots, it's quite a deed.

A fox in a hat, oh what a sight,
Tells a joke that feels just right.
The trees all laugh, their leaves a-shake,
In this wooded world, joy's awake.

Echoes Beneath the Canopy

Under branches, whispers play,
Woodpeckers tap in a funny way.
Their rhythm's off, but hearts are light,
As-chipmunks dance through day and night.

Mice wear glasses, read the stars,
While raccoons debate their candy bars.
"Oh dear, where's the sweet on my shelf?"
They laugh aloud, then eat themselves.

The breeze brings tales from ages past,
Of frogs in hats, with joy amassed.
Their croaks a chorus of silly tunes,
In this woods where whimsy balloons.

A porcupine sports a flashy tie,
He wobbles forth, then gives a sigh.
"Too fancy for me!" he starts to frown,
Then slips and rolls all the way down.

Secrets of the Ancient Grove

Old trees chuckle, holding secrets tight,
Whispers of laughter filter through the night.
A wise old owl surveys the scene,
With spectacles on, he's quite the keen.

Squirrels trade jokes, crafting their tales,
While weaving through brambles, dodging their trails.
"Why did the crow sit on the wire?"
"Well, he was too fat to fly any higher!"

Beneath the ferns, a hedgehog snores,
Dreaming of donuts and wooden floors.
"Who ordered breakfast on a plate?"
He mutters aloud, "It's quite a fate!"

In the grove, with giggles not rare,
Even the mushrooms chuckle and stare.
Nature's stage, a comical show,
Where every leaf has something to sow.

Shadows Between the Trees

In shadows deep, where giggles reign,
A raccoon juggles berries with no disdain.
"Timber-who? Just call me a star!"
He trips and spills his snacks from afar.

The deer don hats, then prance about,
With each graceful leap, they twist and shout.
"Look at us!" they cry, with glee,
As branches sway, it's quite the spree.

A gossiping crow shares the latest news,
About a bear who wore bright blue shoes.
"Such a fashion faux pas!" caws the spry,
But the bear walks by, waving, oh my!

With shadows dancing, laughter explodes,
In a world of whimsy, where joy erodes.
The forest thrives in the silliest ways,
Sprinkling fun through all of our days.

Fables Fluttering on the Breezes

In the forest, squirrels conspire,
To steal acorns, they never tire.
A wise old owl just shakes his head,
As chipmunk ninjas make off with bread.

The raccoons in masks, they plot with glee,
In night-time capers, wild and free.
A mischief of foxes, they prance and play,
Chasing their tails till the break of day.

The Canvas of the Canopy

The trees wear hats of leaves so bright,
While birds wear crowns that gleam with light.
A parrot tries a tango dance,
As branches sway in a woodsy trance.

A painter's brush, the sunset spills,
As critters gather for evening thrills.
They laugh and sing beneath the moon,
In a woodland ball that ends too soon.

Rustic Recollections of the Resilient Woods

A bear with a cap, thinks he can skate,
But tumbles headfirst—oh, isn't it great?
The rabbits cheer from a leafy stand,
As he rolls and spins, not quite as planned.

A porcupine's quills make a perfect roof,
While ducks tell tales that dance and goof.
They giggle together on a log so wide,
Sharing whispers of the playful tide.

The Tapestry of Twisted Branches

The vines are tangled, a riddle to solve,
Where mice play games, they're eager to evolve.
A wind that giggles, a breeze that sighs,
Tickles the leaves, as laughter flies.

A party of ants, they march in a line,
Carrying breadcrumbs, they think it's divine.
With a twist and a twirl, the critters all dance,
While the moonlight grins at their silly prance.

Riddles in the Rain

In the forest, drops tap dance,
Where squirrels wear hats, not by chance.
A turtle sings, oh what a sight,
While frogs in tuxedos jump with delight.

Raindrops giggle as they fall,
Each puddle a mirror, reflecting it all.
The trees, they whisper, 'Come have some fun,'
As mushrooms nod, saying, 'We're number one!'

Prose of the Pathless Wood

Once a raccoon tried to be a chef,
But burnt the berries—oh what a mess!
A fox with a quill wrote stories so grand,
But the paper was leaves, and they were unplanned.

The owl just hooted, not quite amused,
While rabbits debated which stories to use.
In this wild realm with such silly ways,
Every wrong turn spins laughable days.

Hidden Stories of the Hollow

A badger once slipped, fell into a stew,
Charmed by the flavors, he invited a crew.
With critters all gathered, they feasted that night,
Except for the skunk, who fled in fright.

The trees stood guard, with their branches all wide,
As laughter erupted, bursting with pride.
In the hollow, where stories collide,
Even the shyest take a fun ride.

The Gossamer Threads of the Glade

In the glade, where the spiders weave tales,
A mouse found a scarf, adorned with big scales.
He wore it with flair, a dandy quite rare,
While bees buzzing loudly thought he was a bear.

Leaves twirled around, making music so spry,
As deer pranced about, lifting spirits up high.
With each silly step, joy took to the air,
In this mystical place, laughter's everywhere.

Beneath the Boughs of Time

In the woods where shadows play,
The squirrels dance in disarray.
One trips over a knotted vine,
And blames a bird for crossing the line.

The raccoons steal from picnic tables,
Whispering plots like fabled fables.
A mouse shouts, 'I've got the cheese!'
While everyone sings, 'Just say please!'

A wise old owl, perched up high,
Claims he's seen a flying pie.
With giggles echoing through the trees,
The squirrels hold a pie-eating spree!

But when they find a pie that's baked,
Turns out it's just a cake that's flaked.
They laugh and roll upon the ground,
In the boughs, pure joy is found.

In the Embrace of Evergreen

Under branches thick and green,
A raccoon puts on a cap unseen.
With a monocle that's cracked in size,
He claims he's wise, oh what a surprise!

The chipmunks join in a conga line,
While the owls hoot, 'Ain't this divine?'
They set up games of hide and seek,
With giggling echoes from peak to peak.

A parrot squawks, 'Let's play charades!'
As laughter dances through the glades.
But when a fox gets hurt in the game,
He cries, "Foul play!" and blames the fame!

Between the trees, humor abounds,
With tales that twist and laughter resounds.
All under the watch of the evergreens,
Life unfolds in quirky scenes.

The Enigma of the Woodland Spirits

In the woods, a riddle spins,
What do spirits think of sins?
The fairies giggle, up in the air,
As they toss acorns without a care.

A gnome claims to know every plot,
But forgets where he put his tot.
'Twas here, he swears, in the big oak tree,
But his hat is now a nest for a bee!

The pixies throw a quirky feast,
Inviting creatures from west to east.
But when the food turns out to be grass,
They wear it well and all laugh en masse.

A wise old tree hums low and deep,
Cracking jokes that make the forest leap.
With humor sewn in every seam,
The woodland spirits giggle and dream.

Starlit Stories Overhead

Beneath the stars, a tale unfolds,
Of creatures daring, brave, and bold.
A beaver builds a boat of cheese,
While frogs discuss their fashion keys.

An owl says, "I saw a sight!"
"A raccoon dressed in silver light!"
But just then it tumbles down the hill,
In a flash of fur and giggles, what a thrill!

Fireflies twinkle, setting the mood,
While beetles tap their feet in the wood.
The moon chuckles at the scenes he sees,
As laughter sways on the evening breeze.

So gather round, you critters, come,
With stories shared and laughter hum.
In starlit glow, so wild and free,
The night becomes a jubilee!

The Rhythm of Rustling Leaves

Leaves chatter in the breeze,
Squirrels dance with awkward ease.
A raccoon slips in broad daylight,
Wearing acorns like a hat, what a sight!

Branches sway with goofy grins,
Woodpeckers make their loud violins.
The wind hums, a silly tune,
While chipmunks twirl, under the moon.

Frogs leap high, perform a show,
While ants march in a row, oh so slow!
Nature's circus, wild and free,
Just look at that tree, root's got glee!

Dancing beetles spin around,
In rhythm with a bouncy sound.
Nature's laughter fills the air,
Join the fun, if you dare!

Chronicles of the Silent Pines

Among the pines, whispers joke,
One tree shivers, starts to poke.
A fox strolls by in snickered plight,
With paws too big, he tumbles, what a sight!

Twisted trunks play peek-a-boo,
Squirrels plotting, what to do?
They hide their nuts in secret stashes,
But the crow caws; they'll face some crashes!

A turtle moves at an easy pace,
Challenged by a quick rat race.
But slow and steady wins the day,
While boastful critters fade away.

The trees chuckle, leaves a-flutter,
As the winds weave tales, now that's the utter!
In this forest, funny and grand,
All creatures share a light-hearted brand!

A Journey Through Verdant Glades

Through the glades, we skip and hop,
Where giggling blooms make joy nonstop.
A badger rolls, too round to flee,
With wrinkles and chuckles, can't you see?

Sunlight spills like warm honey,
Where ladybugs play, isn't that funny?
A bramble patch turns into a nest,
With a hedgehog snoozing, he's on a quest!

Frolicsome fawns chase their tails,
While buzzards swoop with gossiping gales.
Oh, what a sight, a ruckus instead,
In the land where laughter is widely spread!

Pattering paws, a joyous din,
Where the fun starts, let the day begin!
Nature's playground, wild yet nice,
Every step holds a sweet surprise!

The Lullaby of the Stream

Bubbling brook with whispers soft,
Carries tales as it rushes aloft.
Fish jump high, it's a watery play,
Each splash and giggle brightens the day.

Frogs croak songs of silly dreams,
While the current tosses bright sunbeams.
Otters slide down muddy banks,
With splashes that earn them all the pranks!

Herons strut like they own the scene,
While fish hide out, they're not so keen.
Bubbles rise with each playful splash,
As nature sings in a cheerful clash.

So come along, let the stream be your guide,
To the land where joy and silliness abide.
With every ripple, a chuckle abounds,
In this laughter-filled world, fun resounds!

Footprints in the Forest Floor

In the woods, a squirrel wore shoes,
Chasing shadows, dodging a moose.
A raccoon danced in pajamas bright,
While birds threw acorns with all their might.

Footprints left from a wobbly ant,
Scribbled tales of a woodland chant.
A fox in a hat, with style and flair,
Declared the woods a grand affair.

Reflections on the Riverbank

A fish flipped tales of a splashing spree,
While frogs croaked jokes beneath a tree.
The river giggled, bubbles afloat,
As ducks quacked puns in a comic boat.

Cattails swayed with a sassy beat,
The turtles joined, making merry at their feet.
Sun glistened bright on the water's grin,
As the reeds whispered secrets of the din.

Beneath the Veil of Vines

Vines tangled up in a messy twist,
"Who tied this knot?" a chipmunk hissed.
A rabbit snickered, not one to miss,
"It's a jungle gym of pure bliss!"

The leaves above were a giggling choir,
As lizards slid down, getting a flyer.
Twisting and turning, they formed a line,
"Who knew the forest could dance so fine?"

Songs of the Serene Stream

The stream hummed softly, a melody sweet,
While rocks played maracas in quirky beat.
A beaver with rhythm tapped on a log,
Brought ants to the stage for a funky jog.

Water lilies clapped, a floral parade,
With dragonflies buzzing, they swayed and swayed.
"Join us, dear critters!" the streams did implore,
"Let's party all night till the sun hits the shore!"

A Serenade in Sapwood

In a forest where trees like to dance,
A squirrel in tights took a chance.
He twirled and he spun, with a joyful shout,
While birds watched in awe, unable to doubt.

The mossy old oak let out a chuckle,
As the beavers all joined in a huddle.
They whittled away at a log for a fluke,
While frogs croaked in time to the joyous croon.

A raccoon on stage wore a shiny bow,
And put on a show with a glance and a show.
With acorns for maracas, they could not stop,
The merriment flowed like a sugary pop.

As the moon beamed down through branches so spry,
The wind made them giggle, oh my, oh my!
They sang of the sapwood, of laughter, of glee,
In a goofy old forest that's wild and free.

Cartography of the Canopy

In the canopy high, where the branches twist,
A bird made a map, oh what a tryst!
With a crayon beak, he drew funny sights,
Of treehouse castles and mushroom knights.

A raccoon brought snacks, said, 'What a surprise!'
He opened a box of the best hazelnuts pies.
While owls hooted loudly, keeping a score,
A rabbit did cartwheels, then asked for some more.

The trees held their breath, with the sun shining bright,
As branches took part in this whimsical flight.
With each little branch, a new route unfurled,
Mapping out laughter in this silly old world.

They plotted a course through the gigglewood glade,
Where laughter and fun never ever would fade.
And wherever they traveled, one message was clear:
In the heights of the woods, there's nothing to fear!

The Legend of the Lichen

Once in a grove, where the sunlight peeks,
Lived lichen who spoke in the softest of squeaks.
Each color a tale of the rain and the dew,
They'd giggle and wiggle, with whispers so true.

A legend grew wild of their secret clan,
Of dancing beneath, where the tall grasses ran.
With cheeky old toads as their front-row fans,
They'd pickle and dance in their mossy prance.

When a breeze would arrive, they'd tremble with glee,
For stories of mischief drifted down from the tree.
And under the moon, with a shimmer so bright,
They'd celebrate life through the deep of the night.

No tale was too silly, no whimsy too grand,
As they twinkled and tickled the soft, silted sand.
For the legend of lichen will always be fun,
Where nature composes its kind-hearted pun.

Stillness Amidst the Timbers

In stillness where silence would often abide,
A bear held a party, though no one could hide.
With berries and honey, he set up a feast,
Inviting all critters, both greatest and least.

A turtle in slippers came plodding along,
While a porcupine hummed a sweet little song.
They danced on the leaves with a jittery flop,
And laughed till they fell, never wanting to stop.

A woodpecker knocked, saying 'What's going on?'
He joined in the fun, tapping out a raucous song.
As the sun kissed the trees, they wiggled and spun,
Mirrors of laughter reflected this fun.

As twilight approached, their giggles still thrived,
In stillness, a spell of pure joy had arrived.
With critters and laughter and food all around,
In the heart of the woods, happiness found.

The Heartbeat of the Forest

In the woods where the squirrels chat,
A raccoon wore a fancy hat.
He danced with bees, a sight to see,
While owls hooted, chuckling with glee.

A tree once tried to tell a joke,
But all the leaf-lovers just choked.
The pinecones giggled, the brambles swayed,
As the forest's heartbeat played.

A breeze would swirl and lift the leaves,
As laughter echoed, no one grieves.
A porcupine with quite the quirk,
Told tall tales of his wild work.

Now every critter sings along,
To the rhythm of this woodland song.
Life's absurdity brings forth cheer,
In the trees where humor's near.

Stories Woven in Bark

Bark beetles laughed with such delight,
Telling stories through the night.
A wise old owl perched high above,
Could barely keep up with all the love.

Mice wore capes, playing superhero,
While chipmunks raced their tiny hero.
They'd scurry fast to gain the prize,
A crumb of cheese, oh what a surprise!

Frogs would croak in a comic way,
Imitating the squirrel's ballet.
The willows whispered, 'What a scene!'
As the forest joined the playful theme.

But the best tales spun on the breeze,
Carried along by playful trees.
Life's punchlines grew like tangled vines,
In this woodland where laughter shines.

Legends Carved in Roots

Deep in the earth, where secrets lie,
The roots would chatter, oh so spry.
Tales of giants who danced with glee,
And bees who brewed the finest tea.

A hickory laughed with a booming sound,
As acorns rolled across the ground.
Roots tangled in humorous plots,
Of ladybugs and their silly dots.

The earthworms cracked jokes, oh so grand,
Creating snickers across the land.
One claimed to be a dinosaur,
Until a robin said, 'Not anymore!'

This underground world was rife with fun,
As laughter echoed, no need to run.
The legends grew with each twist and turn,
In the depths where the roots still yearn.

Moonlight Over Mossy Trails

Under the moon, on trails so bright,
The critters gathered for a night.
A fox recited rhymes with flair,
While a raccoon combed his messy hair.

The moss wore shoes made of silver dew,
As the glowworms twinkled, forming a crew.
A frog donned shades, claiming his cool,
Holding court like a nighttime school.

The shadows danced in a merry jig,
As fireflies lit the way so big.
A bear tried to waltz, with two left feet,
The forest erupted in laughter sweet.

In this moonlit glow, joy takes flight,
Each creature revels in the night.
While the trails whisper secrets anew,
Under moonlight, fun's in full view.

The Enchanted Glade

In a glade where the squirrels play,
The rabbits hop and dance all day.
With acorn hats upon their heads,
They tease the fox in fun-filled threads.

A turtle races with a hare,
But all the while, he just eats air!
The birds chirp songs of silly lore,
While the bear snores loud, what a snore!

Old raccoons tell tales of fluff,
Of shiny things, they've got enough.
The flowers giggle in the breeze,
Making friends with buzzing bees.

And when the sun begins to dip,
The fireflies join in for a trip.
A party starts with laughter bright,
In the glade, all feels just right!

Rustling Leaves and Hidden Paths

Through hidden paths where wild things roam,
There's a raccoon who's lost his home.
He wears a map that's upside down,
And wonders where he left his crown.

The wind whispers secrets in the trees,
As chipmunks argue over cheese.
One squirrel brings a pie to share,
But ends up sitting in a chair!

They've held a feast of nuts and fun,
While crow steals cookies on the run.
In rustling leaves, they laugh and shout,
For every corner holds a clout.

But when the sun begins to set,
The critters gather, no regret.
In shadows long, they bid goodnight,
For tomorrow brings more silly sights!

Serpents Through the Saplings

In the thicket hide the snakes,
With all their pranks and silly shakes.
They wriggle through the brush with glee,
Playing tricks on a busy bee.

A mischievous one plans a show,
With a leaf for a hat, off he goes!
But tangled up in a silly vine,
He smiles and asks, "Is this divine?"

The smart little frog joins the fun,
Jumping high beneath the sun.
They laugh so hard, they start to roll,
In garlands made of twigs, how bold!

Amidst the trees, the laughter swells,
As creatures share their funny tales.
No one's afraid in this green land,
Where every critter lends a hand!

Moonlit Meadows and Gnarled Roots

In moonlit meadows, shadows play,
Where creatures come out to sway and stay.
The owls hoot with a comical flair,
As fireflies buzz without a care.

A hedgehog wears a fancy coat,
While dancing daintily, takes a note.
The rabbits join with leaps so grand,
They create a conga line, so planned!

The gnarled roots, they tap their toes,
While wise old trees share ticklish prose.
Each rustle brings a giggle near,
In the meadow, there's nothing to fear.

As night unfolds, they sing a tune,
Beneath the bright and gleeful moon.
In this lively, joyous parade,
All creatures love the games they've made!

The Dance of Dappled Sunlight

In a grove where shadows prance,
Sunbeams twirl, they love to dance.
Squirrels giggle, branch to branch,
Chasing rays, they take a chance.

The leaves are clapping with delight,
As crickets sing with all their might.
A rabbit hops, a jolly sight,
In this golden morning light.

A bear attempts a wobbly spin,
But tumbles down, a fluffy win.
A chorus of chuckles from within,
As nature laughs, let fun begin.

With every twirl, with every gleam,
The forest plays a joyful theme.
In sunshine's arms, we dare to dream,
Life can be quite the funny scheme.

Murmurs of the Wildflower Meadow

Flowers gossip in the breeze,
Tickled petals, buzzing bees.
A dandelion shares a joke,
While daisies giggle, 'Oh, what a poke!'

Butterflies flaunt their silly styles,
Flitting 'round and flashing smiles.
A tulip trips, then starts to sway,
And stammers, 'Oh, what a clumsy day!'

The grass grows tall, then takes a bow,
While a bumblebee asks, 'What's now?'
Pansies nod, in colors bright,
Joining in with sheer delight.

In this meadow, laughter blooms,
With every joke, joy resumes.
Nature's humor finds its rooms,
Amidst wildflowers' bright costumes.

The Echoing Footfalls of Nature

A deer tiptoes, oh so sly,
With a squirrel who gives a sigh.
'This forest floor, so full of sounds,
Bounces back in leaps and bounds!'

From ragged rocks, the echoes play,
As frogs croak puns, hip-hip-hooray!
A raccoon slips, his footfalls loud,
And chuckles form a teasing crowd.

Birds chirp jokes with winged delight,
As shadows waltz through day and night.
Nature's rhythm, such a delight,
In every corner, laughter's bright.

Who knew a stroll could bring such cheer?
With every echo, joy is near.
The footfalls ring, let's give a cheer,
For all the giggles we hold dear!

Whims of the Wandering Wind

A breeze whizzes, with a wink,
Rustles leaves that start to think.
'What mischief next?' they softly muse,
As wind plays tricks, it steers and cruise.

Through the branches, it sneaks and sways,
Chasing thoughts in curious ways.
A gust spirals and tickles the air,
While trees giggle with a cheerful flair.

A tumbleweed joins the ballet,
Rolling 'round in a playful way.
Wind whispers puns that make trees laugh,
In leafy whispers, it drafts its path.

Each twist and turn, a breezy jest,
The wandering air knows how to jest.
In nature's play, it's truly blessed,
With laughter woven, it's the best!

Guardians of the Great Green

In a forest, tall and wide,
Squirrels dance with great pride.
They guard trees, both old and new,
Chasing shadows, a lively crew.

A raccoon sings, a frog does clap,
While owls giggle, a sneaky trap.
With acorns flying, they share a jest,
Oh, what fun in their leafy nest!

But watch your step when laughter soars,
For tree roots hide like playful paws.
The guardians laugh as you trip and fall,
In this raucous woods, they have a ball!

So join the fun, don't miss a beat,
Dance with critters on tiny feet.
In the great green, life's a hoot,
Where laughter echoes, and joy takes root.

A Symphony in the Sap

Beneath the boughs, the music swells,
Woodpeckers drum, oh how it yells!
Sap flows gently, like a sweet tune,
Nature's choir sings to the moon.

A badger strums on a twiggy harp,
As chipmunks hum, weaving the art.
The melody dances on gentle breeze,
And jumping frogs join with ease.

Bees buzz softly, a buzzing song,
While branches sway, they all belong.
A cacophony of giggles ring,
In the heart of the woods, the critters swing!

So gather 'round, let's make a noise,
In this forest filled with joys.
For in each drop of sticky sap,
Lies a melody of nature's map.

Journey Through Mossy Realms

Step lightly on the spongy floor,
Where fairies hide and giggle more.
Mossy carpets, emerald hue,
Guide you to worlds both strange and true.

A snail on a mission, oh so slow,
With grand ideas, he puts on a show.
He boasts of treasures under logs,
While sly raccoons plan pranks, the rogues!

Glimpses of light, through branches peek,
As squirrels chatter, their conversations leak.
"Did you hear that?" one squeaks in thrill,
"Worms are dancing on yonder hill!"

So wander down these mossy trails,
Where laughter rings and mischief sails.
Each twist and turn brings more delight,
In this whimsical wood, all feels just right.

Noble Giants in Slumber

Tall trees sleep, with dreams so grand,
While critters gather, a merry band.
Debates about acorns and the best nuts,
They plot and scheme with little struts.

A wise old owl, though half asleep,
Giggles softly, secrets to keep.
"Why did the tree cross the path?" he snorts,
"To leaf a message for all sorts!"

As shadows stretch, the stories weave,
Of giggling leaves that trick and deceive.
The squirrels concoct their playful schemes,
In the night's hush, they chase wild dreams.

With whispers of laughter, the forest glows,
As noble giants in slumber doze.
In their embrace, mischief does creep,
While the woods giggle softly, drifting to sleep.

Howls Beneath Hardwood

A squirrel in a cap, so bright,
Dances on branches, what a sight!
He drops acorns, oh what a mess,
Sings to the moon in his fuzzy dress.

A raccoon joins, with a sly little grin,
Claiming the snacks that the critters begin.
They pull at the roots, causing a fuss,
In the shadowy wood, they laugh at us.

Trees twisted like pretzels, oh my!
With limbs that reach out, they seem to sigh.
"Don't blame us, we just provide shade,
While the woodland antics are gladly displayed."

When night falls soft and shadows dance,
The critters in laughter, they take their chance.
Under the stars with giggles that swell,
The hardwood's a stage, it knows it too well.

The Sonnet of the Starlit Lebore

A firefly party, in joyful parade,
With flashes and twinkles, a spectacle made.
The frogs croak in harmony, a bass line so deep,
As crickets contribute, their chirps never sleep.

The owl looks puzzled, "What's all this cheer?"
As the raccoon brings snacks, grinning ear to ear.
"Who invited the possum?" the hedgehog complains,
But the moon says, "Stay put, let's loosen our chains!"

A dance breaks out, on the soft mossy ground,
With rabbits in bowties, all jumping around.
The stars overhead twinkle in delight,
At the woodland shindig, oh what a sight!

As dawn draws near, the revelers sigh,
"We'll meet again, under this sky!"
With promises made in the morning's warm light,
The funny old forest bids us goodnight.

Chronicles Carved in Stone

In the shadows of rocks, tales twist and bend,
Where chipmunks tell stories that never quite end.
"There once was a fox, quite clever and spry,
Who wore fancy boots and could leap very high."

The turtles all chuckle, "We saw him last week,
Stuck in a puddle, oh what a peak!"
With a splash and a giggle, he gave quite a show,
While the snails took their time, "We will take it slow."

Gravestones of laughter, in nature's great tome,
Where laughter is echoed, and friendships feel home.
The boulders all whisper, "This life is a rhyme,
In the woodland's great stories, we find our own time."

So gather your joys, let your laughter roam,
Under the boughs where the wild things call home.
For the chronicles live in our hearts oh so deep,
Where even the starlings their secrets will keep.

The Path Beyond the Pines

Upon the trail where the pine trees sway,
A weasel in glasses declares, "Let's play!"
He spins little tales of the things that he's seen,
As the mice all take notes from their spots in between.

"Don't follow that rabbit, he's off to the show,
With a script and a hat, and a flair for the flow!"
The woods come alive with a giggle and cheer,
As the antics of animals bring joy far and near.

A bear with a top hat and a cane made of bark,
Leads the parade down, through the glade where it's dark.
"Let's dance by the stream!" he calls out with a roar,
And the critters reply, "We'll dance evermore!"

With twirls and with leaps, the stars in their grace,
Celebrate friendship in this whimsical space.
For in the heart of the woods, all's well and divine,
In the laughter and joy along the path through the pines.

The Fables of Forgotten Branches

In the woods where the squirrels plot,
A raccoon with a clever thought,
Wore a hat made of leaves and twigs,
And danced with the frogs and the jigs.

The owls hooted, their laughter loud,
As they gathered a giggling crowd,
While the bunnies hopped, a comical sight,
Chasing fireflies into the night.

A beaver built a wacky dam,
Out of sticks and an old tin can,
He claimed it was a palace fine,
But woodchucks said, 'That's just a line!'

So here in this land of delight,
Where trees have secrets, out of sight,
Every branch has a story to tell,
Of laughter and glee, oh so well!

Frolics in the Fern-filled Forest

In a glen where the ferns stand tall,
A gopher threw a crazy ball,
He aimed it at a dizzy bee,
Who loop-de-looped with glee, oh me!

A frog in a crown, quite the sight,
Decided to dance with all his might,
Twisting and turning, lost in fun,
While crickets chirped, 'You're number one!'

A turtle in shades, moving slow,
Claimed he could race, much to our woe,
But he tripped on a root, oh so fun,
And bumped the squirrel who yelled, 'Not done!'

Through giggles and shrieks that never end,
The forest is where we all can blend,
With laughter in leaves and stories galore,
In this fern-filled land, who could ask for more?

Chronicles of Nature's Architects

The beaver donned a builder's hat,
And called on a raccoon for a chat,
'Let's make a fort of wood and mud,
And throw a party in the flood!'

The ants all marched with tiny might,
Carrying crumbs, what a sight,
They'd play the drums with acorn caps,
While nearby, the fireflies clapped.

A woodpecker knocked a beat so bright,
He challenged a squirrel to a fight,
But both burst out in silly glee,
When they tripped o'er roots by a tree.

In nature's hands, fun takes flight,
With creatures dancing, hearts so light,
Each twist and turn, a whimsical cheer,
In the forest, laughter draws near.

Oak Leaves and Morning Dew

Under oak leaves, a party brewed,
Where gnomes did sashay, yes, it's true,
With laughter ringing through the air,
A hiccup here, a jaunty flair.

A cat and a dog played peek-a-boo,
Their antics made the whole crew woo,
While butterflies joined in the game,
Stirring up giggles, never the same.

The morning dew held a twinkle bright,
A crystal ball of sheer delight,
Where toads sang tunes, not a bore,
And everyone laughed until they were sore.

So come to the shade of the oak so grand,
With joy and silliness all so planned,
In this realm, where fun's the decree,
We'll dance in the dew, wild and free!

Echoes of the Evergreen

In a pine tree party, the squirrels play,
Dancing 'round the branches, come what may.
Raccoons in tuxedos, so very sly,
Peer through the leaves with a curious eye.

The owls are hooting, wearing big hats,
While chipmunks sing songs, making all the chats.
A bear with a banjo strums a silly tune,
As the wind whispers secrets under the moon.

The deer do the cha-cha, the fox leads the line,
Each creature's got moves that are simply divine.
With giggles and laughter, the woods come alive,
In this grand forest bash, everybody can thrive.

When the sun starts to set, they all take a bow,
Grateful for moments, oh, the fun they allow.
As shadows stretch long, they bid their goodbyes,
With hearts full of joy, beneath starlit skies.

Shadows of the Silent Grove

Beneath leafy canopies, giggles abound,
Where whispers of mischief are always found.
A raccoon in sunglasses, what a sight to see,
Playing tricks on the owl, just as happy as can be.

The mice have a race, on tiny little wheels,
Their squeaks echo softly, oh, what fun feels!
While frogs in red coats leap from a log,
Challenging the crickets to a carefree jog.

The trees wear a smile, with branches that sway,
As squirrels tell jokes in their cheeky way.
The deer roll their eyes, in a playful stance,
In this grove of shadows, they all take a chance.

When moonlight spills over, the giggles will burst,
For laughter in silence has quenched their thirst.
And they close the night's tale with a soft little cheer,
In the shadows of stillness, joy always is near.

The Heartbeat of the Forest

In a forest so lively, the creatures unite,
With squirrels on stilts, it's a marvelous sight.
Owls are the judges, with a wink and a nod,
As fawns spin around like a graceful facade.

The badgers hold lanterns, gleaming so bright,
Directing the dance through the magical night.
The raccoon tells stories, with flair and with glee,
About all the antics that happened last week.

The river joins in, with a bubbling cheer,
As frogs leap along, their voices sincere.
A porcupine juggles while standing on paws,
And everyone gasps, then erupts into applause.

As dawn starts to break, and the moon fades away,
They hoot and they howl, for they've had their say.
In the heart of the woods, friendship is found,
With the pulse of the forest, where laughter is sound.

Chronicles of the Ancient Oaks

Under ancient oaks, where the branches tickle,
The acorns are rolling, and everyone giggles.
The tortoise tripped over his own two feet,
While a parrot squawks jokes, oh, isn't that sweet?

A hedgehog in glasses reads tales of the past,
While the rabbits debate which snack will last.
A party of fish splashes all around,
As they leap for the insects, quite joyfully found.

Generations of whispers in the rustling leaves,
Hold secrets of laughter, and what one believes.
The wise old crow caws, "Join in the fun,
In a world full of wonders, we're never done!"

As the sky turns to dusk, with a glorious flair,
They all gather close, wrapping warmth in the air.
In the chronicles told by the ancient tall trees,
Lies a happiness woven with the softest of breezes.

The Dance of the Dappled Sun

In the woods where squirrels prance,
A spotlight beams in a leafy dance,
Rabbits stomp with furry flair,
While chipmunks twist without a care.

The shadows leap, the sunlight giggles,
As trees perform their swaying wiggles,
A jolly breeze stirs up some fun,
In this merry map of dappled sun.

The flowers spin with petals wide,
While birds whistle along with pride,
A caterpillar takes the lead,
In a conga line—Oh, what a creed!

So join the bash beneath the leaves,
With laughter sprouting, none let's grieve,
For in this fest, we've found our flow,
In a woodland shindig, stealing the show.

Legends of the Lost Leaves

In autumn hills, the leaves confide,
Of wild adventures, side by side,
A crow once claimed a leaf parade,
Wearing one as a hat he'd made.

A squirrel, bold, took to the ground,
To win a race that shook the town,
With acorns flying, laughter rolled,
As every story, now retold.

The whispers tell of dance and song,
When breezes blew, and trees sang strong,
A chipmunk jived, he'd shout, "Hooray!"
In legends steeped, they prance and sway.

So gather 'round with fires bright,
And hear the tales of pure delight,
For in this wood where laughter weaves,
Are legends spun from lost, bright leaves.

Starlight Over the Timberline

As evening falls, the stars all wink,
Around the fire, the critters think,
A raccoon juggles berries small,
While owls watch from the treetops tall.

The fireflies twinkle, a dazzling show,
While bushes rustle, as laughter flows,
A fox in shades does a moonlit flip,
And all the birds join in for a quip.

The night is young, the fun's in full swing,
With stories spun, let the laughter ring,
A bear, he trips, and rolls with glee,
And everyone roars, "Oh, look at he!"

Under starlit skies, the woods in cheer,
With woodland friends, there's naught to fear,
In this grand night, with heartfelt grace,
The timberline holds a joyous space.

Ember Eyes in the Woodland Wild

In shadows deep, with eyes aglow,
The creatures peek, in sets of two or four,
A fox with mischief in his stride,
Leads a band of critters, side by side.

An owl once teased, in ghostly flight,
Dropping twigs with a wink that night,
A bear, bemused, stood up to dance,
And birthed a jig, a chance romance!

The rabbits prance with noses high,
While fireflies whir in the midnight sky,
Each rustle carries giggles soft,
In woodland revelry, spirits loft.

So here beneath the burning glow,
Where ember eyes make magic grow,
With laughter shared, where wild hearts blend,
In nature's embrace, there's joy without end.

Embers of the Forest Floor

In the woods where the shadows dance,
A squirrel tried its luck for a chance.
It tripped on a root, oh what a sight!
Tumbling down, it gave a small fright!

A rabbit laughed, rolling on the ground,
While the owl just hooted, 'I'm wisdom bound!'
The trees all chuckled, their leaves in a spin,
As the furry folks jostled, that was the win!

A chipmunk stashed acorns, a little too bold,
Lost his stash when a bear did unfold.
"Hey buddy!" he squeaked, "You're eating my stash!"
"Just sharing," said bear, with an innocent flash!

As twilight fell and the stars peeked through,
The forest echoed, "Who's sharing stew?"
A soirée of critters, with snacks a delight,
In the heart of the woods, who'd dare say goodnight?

The Soliloquy of Swaying Branches

The branches sway, having their say,
'We're way too tall, come join the play!'
They whispered secrets of what they've seen,
Of cheeky raccoons, so sly and keen.

A beetle then hollered, a self-proclaimed star,
"I'll roll this acorn just to go far!"
The branches chuckled, shaking with glee,
"Careful now, who's watching? Up there, that tree!"

A breeze whispered softly, passing the news,
'It's hard to prank when you have big shoes!'
So the branches plotted, of fun and mischief,
As shadows danced on the forest's cliff.

And with a loud creak, they orchestrated fun,
A leaf-drop party under the sun!
The critters joined in, laughter galore,
In the sway of the branches, who could ask for more?

Prints of the Lost and Found

Footprints scattered across the dirt,
Whose big fuzzy paws, they surely alert!
A raccoon's mischief? Oh, what a mess!
Searching for snacks with some finesse!

Then there's the rabbit with hops so wide,
His leaping left traces of joy and pride.
"Found a carrot!" he shouted with glee,
Until a deer snickered, "Try sharing with me!"

Midway there's a trail, oh what's in store?
A bear in the bushes, just food he'll explore!
"Ah! Not my prints!" the rabbit quickly quipped,
Dashing away, he zigzagged and skipped!

On a stroll, the little fox paused to muse,
At every footprint, he'd carefully choose.
"What's gone, who knows? But I like this game!"
With a tail full of jest, he pranced without shame!

The Mystique of the Hidden Hollow

In the hollow, where shadows look bright,
A gopher held meetings, from day to night.
With a top hat made of the finest schmutz,
He reputedly held the quirkiest ruts!

"Who's in for gossip? Oh what a tale!"
Squeaked the critters as they turned to avail.
The hedgehog plopped, "I've heard something grand,
A turtle's slow dance—what a sight so bland!"

And in that spot, where whispers ignite,
The crickets played tunes, oh what a delight!
A jam session formed, with hops and beats,
'Round the hollow, the forest moved its feets!

As laughter rang out and echoed so clear,
The woodland creatures drew ever near.
In the hidden hollow, where secrets unfold,
Life's little wonders are better retold!

Requiem for Fallen Timber

Oh, mighty oak, you took a fall,
The squirrels laugh, they have a ball.
The woodpecker's got a brand new beat,
He's turned your trunk into a drum retreat.

The chipmunks throw a lumber show,
While crickets chirp in a rowdy flow.
You were so grand, now you lie flat,
Beneath the sun where the woodland sat.

The beetles march with tiny boots,
Parading on your old tree roots.
A funeral feast with mushrooms spry,
In honor of you, oh, stump so sky-high!

So here's to you, dear fallen tree,
Your legacy's a comedy!
With every ring, we'll laugh and cheer,
While nature winks, you've disappeared.

Flickering Lights in the Thicket

In the night where the shadows dance,
Fireflies gather for a fleeting chance.
They flicker about with a giggling spree,
Making vague nonsense of branches and brie.

The rabbit's dressed in his Sunday best,
With a top hat perched, he's quite the jest.
He hops and twirls with fervent delight,
As the stars above giggle, shining bright.

The raccoons throw a moonlit bash,
Sneaking snacks with a cheeky flash.
They swig from jars, they munch on pie,
Knocking over lanterns that passersby spy.

Then comes dusk with its cozy hum,
As shadows recede and the laughter's num.
The thicket's alive with a merry cue,
With friends in the night, and laughter anew.

The Call of the Dappled Dawn

When morning breaks with a yawn and a stretch,
The squirrel resumes his frantic fetch.
A dance with shadows across the dew,
As sunlight flirts with leaves so new.

The birds chirp jokes from every tree,
While the pond holds more than meets the eye.
The frogs croak puns in a lilypad choir,
Creating chaos, with laughter they conspire.

Here comes the deer, with a wobble and hop,
Trying to improvise a fancy stop.
But tripping over roots, he lands in a splash,
The water laughs, giving him quite a thrash!

So let the dawn call to all who roam,
In this joyful woodland, we find our home.
With giggles and grins, we greet the light,
As the day unfolds, in pure delight.

Sagas of the Whispering Pines

The pines weave tales in their gentle sway,
Of wedged-in acorns and summer's play.
Their needles whisper secrets of lore,
As the breeze joins in for an encore.

A fox attempts to catch the sun,
Chasing shadows for added fun.
But slips on mushrooms with a shriek,
And laughter echoes, oh so sleek!

The owls at night hold council wise,
Trading puns and witty ties.
They hoot so loud, we can't keep score,
A laughing contest forevermore.

So listen close to the rustling sound,
In the forest alive, friends abound.
Each whisper, a chuckle, in nature's play,
With sagas spun in a light-hearted way.

Folklore of the Ferns

In a forest where ferns often dance,
A squirrel wore shades, took a chance.
He strutted with flair, a true little star,
Claiming the title of woodland czar.

The owls hooted loud, in fits of pure glee,
"Who's that cool dude? I thought it was me!"
But the bushy-tailed prince simply smirked and said,
"I'm the king of the foliage, stay in your bed!"

A rabbit turned pink, from laughing so hard,
He fell in a puddle, his clothes all marred.
"Just look at that rodent, so slick and absurd,
Wearing those shades, like he's truly disturbed!"

With giggles and jokes, the forest would cheer,
For life in the ferns is a joyous frontier.
Each creature would share in the folly of fun,
Under the rays of the warm, golden sun.

The Solitude of the Summit

Atop the high peak where the yodelers roam,
A goat held a concert, the mountains his home.
With a hat and a bow, he began to sing,
Echoes of laughter became his best bling.

The birds joined in, each with a squawk,
While mice tap-danced on a nearby rock.
"Come one, come all! Enjoy this high fête!"
But only the sheep thought it was first-rate.

A wise old bear, with a chuckle so deep,
Said, "Leave me out, I just want my sleep!"
But the summit was loud with a jubilant cheer,
While the goat played his tunes, they all drew near.

With the sun setting low on the musical scene,
The critters united, a true forest theme.
Each creature up there, felt the summit's delight,
Even grumpy old bears danced into the night.

Harmony at the Hollow's Edge

In a hollow where laughter and antics collide,
A raccoon with maracas began to confide.
"Let's have a fiesta under the moonlight,
I'll lead the parade, it's gonna be quite a sight!"

The rabbits brought carrots, the badgers brought pies,
As the soil vibrated with joyous surprise.
With music erupting from every dark nook,
Even the beetles threw styles into the crook.

"Is that a dance?" asked the shy little mole,
"Or just a tumble? Am I losing control?"
"Just let it all go, embrace every trip,
Life's but a party, not a steady ship!"

With songs and with giggles, the hollow did hum,
With a clatter and scatter, the merriment spun.
The creatures of twilight danced all through the night,
At harmony's edge, everything felt just right.

Secrets of the Shaded Path

On a path where the sunbeams twist and twine,
An otter hid secrets, brewed up some fine wine.
"Step right up, folks! It's a special surprise,
I've mixed sweet and sour, a true feast for the eyes!"

The turtles were puzzled, their heads in a spin,
"Are we meant to drink it? Or dive right in?"
But a wise little frog leaped forward with grace,
"Let's try it together, we'll all find our place!"

With laughter and sloshing, they gathered in cheer,
As spills and mishaps turned raucous and clear.
"Who knew shaded paths held such wonders?" they'd say,

As they danced on the lanes through the mist of the day.

So let this be known, in the twilight so bright,
That secrets of fun linger day and night.
For every fine spill and each giggle they tossed,
Made a tapestry rich, where no joy was lost.

www.ingramcontent.com/pod-product-compliance
Lightning Source LLC
Chambersburg PA
CBHW071845160426
43209CB00003B/421